ROASTS

LAKELAND

Lakeland and ACP Magazines Ltd hereby exclude all liability to the extent permitted by law for any errors or omission in this book and for any loss, damage or expense (whether direct or indirect) suffered by a third party relying on any information contained in this book.

This book was created in 2010 for Lakeland by AWW Books, an imprint of Octopus Publishing Group Ltd, based on materials licensed to it by ACP Magazines Ltd, a division of PBL Media Pty Limited.

54 Park St, Sydney
GPO Box 4088, Sydney, NSW 2001
phone (02) 9282 8618; fax (02) 9267 9438
acpbooks@acpmagazines.com.au;
www.acpbooks.com.au

OCTOPUS PUBLISHING GROUP
Design – Chris Bell
Food Director - Pamela Clark

Published for Lakeland in the United Kingdom by Octopus Publishing Group Limited

Endeavour House
189 Shaftesbury Avenue
London WC2H 8JY
United Kingdom
phone + 44 (0) 207 632 5400;
fax + 44 (0) 207 632 5405
aww@octopusbooks.co.uk;
www.octopusbooks.co.uk
www.australian-womens-weekly.com

Printed and bound in China

A catalogue record for this book is available from the British Library.

ISBN 978-1-907428-17-3

The Department of Health advises that eggs should not be consumed raw. This book contains some dishes made with raw or lightly cooked eggs. It is prudent for vulnerable people such as pregnant and nursing mothers, invalids, the elderly, babies and young children to avoid uncooked or lightly cooked dishes made with eggs. Once prepared, these dishes should be kept refrigerated and used promptly.

This book also includes dishes made with nuts and nut derivatives. It is advisable for those with known allergic reactions to nuts and nut derivatives and those who may be potentially vulnerable to these allergies, such as pregnant and nursing mothers, invalids, the elderly, babies and children to avoid dishes made with nuts and nut oils. It is also prudent to check the labels of pre-prepared ingredients for the possible inclusion of nut derivatives.

Some of the recipes in this book have appeared in other publications.

ROASTS

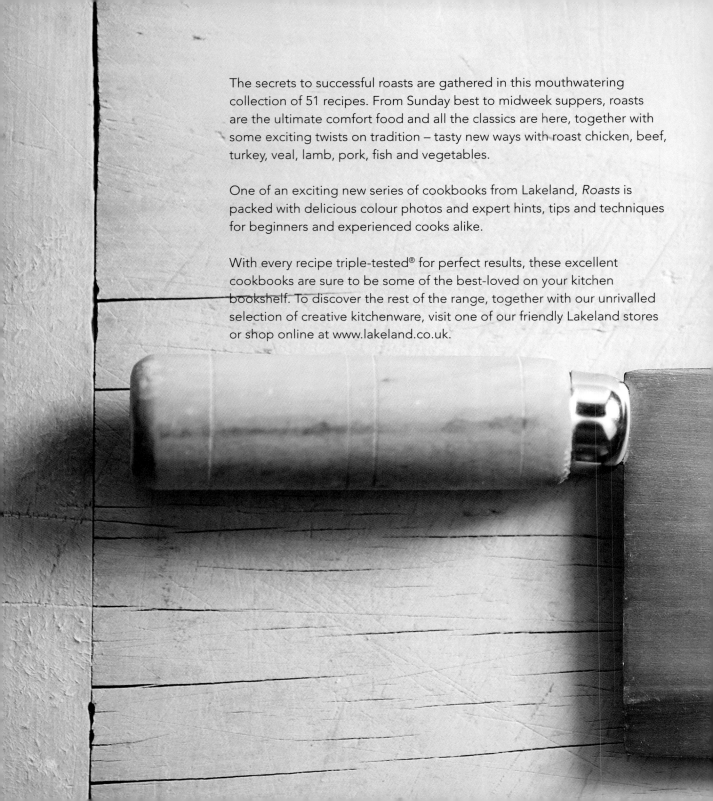

The secrets to successful roasts are gathered in this mouthwatering collection of 51 recipes. From Sunday best to midweek suppers, roasts are the ultimate comfort food and all the classics are here, together with some exciting twists on tradition – tasty new ways with roast chicken, beef, turkey, veal, lamb, pork, fish and vegetables.

One of an exciting new series of cookbooks from Lakeland, *Roasts* is packed with delicious colour photos and expert hints, tips and techniques for beginners and experienced cooks alike.

With every recipe triple-tested® for perfect results, these excellent cookbooks are sure to be some of the best-loved on your kitchen bookshelf. To discover the rest of the range, together with our unrivalled selection of creative kitchenware, visit one of our friendly Lakeland stores or shop online at www.lakeland.co.uk.

CONTENTS

THE PERFECT ROAST

Roasts are a relatively simple affair, but a few shared tips and tricks will guarantee that you get mouthwatering results every time.

ROASTING MEAT

• Remove any silver sinew from a beef fillet to prevent shrinkage and toughening.

• Select a roasting dish large enough to fit the roast; make sure that the meat doesn't extend over the sides of the dish.

• A rack in the roasting dish helps good circulation of heat around the meat.

• The meat should have reached room temperature before you begin cooking.

• When tying a roast, wet the kitchen string first. As the string dries (from the heat of the oven) it will shrink, holding the meat firm.

• Before heating the oven, check that the oven racks are in the right position.

• Meat can be cooked in an oven bag to prevent any spattering and to retain moisture. If you use an oven bag the cooking time might need to be reduced – always follow the instructions on the oven bag packaging.

• Very large cuts of meat will need to be turned halfway through cooking.

• The best way to tell if a roast is done is to use a meat thermometer. Insert the thermometer into the thickest part of the joint, taking care not to touch any bone as this will give you an inaccurate reading. The reading should be 60°C for rare, 70°C for medium and 75°C for well done.

• Take the roast out of the oven and rest it, loosely covered in foil, for 10–15 minutes before carving, to allow the meat juices to 'settle'.

• Carve meat across the grain to ensure tenderness. While carving, hold the meat with tongs, rather than a fork, to prevent juice loss. The best type of knife to use for carving is one with a straight edge, rather than a serrated one.

ROASTING POULTRY

• Before roasting a chicken or turkey wash well in cold water, especially inside the cavity. Pat dry inside and out with absorbent paper.

• Do not freeze an uncooked, stuffed chicken or turkey. The bird and the stuffing can be frozen separately, then thawed, before the bird is stuffed and cooked.

• Fill the cavity loosely with stuffing just before roasting as it will swell during cooking. Secure the cavity closed with cocktail sticks or small skewers. Any leftover stuffing can be moistened with a little stock and cooked in a lightly oiled mini muffin tin. Alternatively, it can be formed into a roll and wrapped in lightly oiled aluminium foil. Bake the extra stuffing with the roast for the last 20 minutes of cooking time.

• Tuck the wing tips under the body and tie the legs together with kitchen string to help a chicken keep its shape during roasting.

• Baste a roast chicken or turkey only occasionally – frequent basting will result in a pale coloured bird.

• To test if a roast chicken or turkey is cooked prick the thigh flesh where it meets the body with a metal skewer. If the juice runs out clear, the bird is cooked.

• If using a frozen turkey, allow up to three days for it to thaw in the fridge.

• To thaw a turkey, cut a small corner off the bag in which it is frozen and place the turkey in a dish. Stand the turkey on a slight angle so that any liquid will drain out of the bag as the turkey defrosts. Discard the liquid from the dish as it accumulates.

• If keeping a cooked chicken or turkey overnight, remove any stuffing from the cavity and refrigerate that separately.

POULTRY

CLASSIC ROAST CHICKEN

1.8kg whole chicken
2 tablespoons olive oil
6 medium potatoes (1kg), halved
2 tablespoons plain flour
500ml chicken stock
250ml water
bacon & leek stuffing
40g butter
2 rashers rindless bacon (130g),
  chopped finely
1 small leek (200g), sliced thinly
2 trimmed celery stalks (200g),
  chopped finely
140g stale breadcrumbs
1 egg, beaten lightly
1 tablespoon coarsely chopped
  fresh sage

1 Preheat oven to 200°C/180°C fan-assisted. Make stuffing.
2 Wash chicken under cold running water; pat dry inside and out with absorbent paper. Tuck wing tips under chicken. Trim skin around neck; secure to underside of chicken with cocktail sticks.
3 Fill cavity with bacon & leek stuffing; tie legs together with string. Place chicken on oiled wire rack in large flameproof baking dish. Rub chicken all over with half the oil; roast, uncovered, 1½ hours.
4 Meanwhile, boil, steam or microwave potato 5 minutes; drain. Combine potato and remaining oil in large shallow baking dish; roast, uncovered, alongside chicken 1 hour, turning occasionally during roasting. Remove chicken from oven; cover to keep warm. Remove and discard cocktail sticks.
5 Increase oven temperature to 240°C/220°C fan-assisted. Roast potato, uncovered, further 15 minutes or until browned and crisp.

6 Meanwhile, drain all but 2 tablespoons of the juices from chicken dish, add flour; cook, stirring over medium heat, until mixture thickens and bubbles. Gradually add combined stock and the water, stirring until gravy boils and thickens. Strain into large jug. Serve with chicken and potatoes.
bacon & leek stuffing Melt butter in medium frying pan; cook bacon, leek and celery until vegetables are tender, cool. Combine bacon mixture in medium bowl with breadcrumbs, egg and sage.

prep + cook time 1 hour 50 minutes (+ cooling)
serves 4
nutritional count per serving
61.3g total fat (20.5g saturated fat); 1046 cal (4320kJ); 56.0g carbohydrate; 65.3g protein; 6.5g fibre

ROAST CHICKEN WITH
RED ONIONS, GARLIC & CHERRIES

1.8kg whole chicken
3 sprigs fresh thyme
½ lemon
10 cloves garlic
30g butter, softened
3 medium red onions (500g),
   cut into wedges
2 tablespoons olive oil
225g fresh cherries

1 Preheat oven to 180°C/160°C fan-assisted.

2 Wash the cavity of the chicken under cold water; pat dry with absorbent paper. Insert two of the thyme sprigs, lemon and two of the garlic cloves into the cavity. Tuck wings under chicken, tie chicken legs together with kitchen string.

3 Place chicken, breast-side up, on oiled wire rack in small roasting dish. Rub chicken all over with softened butter; roast, uncovered, 20 minutes.

4 Combine onion, remaining garlic and oil in medium baking dish. Roast onion mixture alongside chicken further 50 minutes.

5 Add cherries to onion mixture, toss gently to combine; sprinkle remaining thyme over chicken. Roast chicken and cherry mixture further 10 minutes or until chicken is tender and cherries are hot.

prep + cook time 1 hour 40 minutes
serves 4
nutritional count per serving
51.8g total fat (16.7g saturated fat); 707 cal (2955kJ); 11.8g carbohydrate; 47.6g protein; 3.8g fibre

TANDOORI CHICKEN WINGS

16 small chicken wings (1.3kg)
150g tandoori paste
140g natural yogurt
1 medium onion (150g), grated

1 Preheat oven to 220°C/200°C fan-assisted.
2 Cut wings into three pieces at joints; discard tips. Combine chicken and remaining ingredients in large bowl. Cover; refrigerate 3 hours or overnight.
3 Place chicken, in single layer, on oiled wire rack set inside large shallow baking dish. Roast, uncovered, about 30 minutes or until chicken is well browned and cooked through.
4 Serve wings with lime wedges, if desired.

prep + cook time 40 minutes (+ refrigeration)
makes 32
nutritional count per wing
3.0g total fat (0.7g saturated fat); 56 cal (234kJ); 0.8g carbohydrate; 6.4g protein; 0.5g fibre

HARISSA-ROASTED CHICKEN & VEG

1 small orange (180g), cut into thin wedges
1.6kg whole chicken
1 tablespoon olive oil
300g baby onions
1 bulb garlic, separated into cloves, unpeeled
500g baby new potatoes
4 baby aubergines (240g), halved lengthways
250g cherry tomatoes
harissa
15g dried red chillies, chopped coarsely
½ teaspoon ground cumin
½ teaspoon ground coriander
½ teaspoon caraway seeds
1 clove garlic, quartered
1 tablespoon tomato paste
2 teaspoons finely grated orange rind
60ml orange juice

1 Make harissa.
2 Preheat oven to 180°C/160°C fan-assisted.
3 Place orange inside cavity of chicken. Make a pocket between breast and skin with fingers; rub 2 tablespoons of the harissa under skin inside pocket. Tie legs together with kitchen string; brush chicken all over with 2 tablespoons of the harissa.
4 Half-fill large shallow baking dish with water; place chicken on oiled wire rack over dish. Roast, uncovered, about 1 hour. Cover; roast, further 50 minutes or until chicken is cooked through.
5 Meanwhile, heat oil in large flameproof baking dish; cook onions, garlic and potatoes, stirring, until vegetables are browned. Add aubergine and tomatoes; roast in oven for the last 20 minutes of chicken cooking time or until vegetables are tender. Serve with chicken and remaining harissa.

harissa soak chilli in small heatproof bowl of boiling water 1 hour. Drain; reserve 60ml soaking liquid. Dry-fry spices in small heated frying pan until fragrant. Blend or process spices with chilli, reserved liquid, garlic and paste until smooth; transfer to small bowl, stir in rind and juice.

prep + cook time 2 hours 35 minutes (+ standing)
serves 4
nutritional count per serving
37.5g total fat (10.7g saturated fat); 650 cal (2717kJ); 27.9g carbohydrate; 46.1g protein; 8.3g fibre

CHORIZO-STUFFED ROAST CHICKEN

20g butter
1 medium brown onion (150g),
  chopped finely
1 chorizo sausage (170g), diced
  into 1cm pieces
110g stale breadcrumbs
100g ricotta cheese
1 egg
3 tablespoons finely chopped
  fresh flat-leaf parsley
35g roasted slivered almonds
1.6kg whole chicken
2 medium lemons (280g), cut into
  wedges
spinach & red onion salad
150g baby spinach leaves
1 small red onion (100g), sliced
  thinly
1 tablespoon red wine vinegar
2 tablespoons olive oil

1 Melt half of the butter in medium frying pan; cook onion and chorizo, stirring, until onion softens. Cool 10 minutes. Combine chorizo mixture in medium bowl with breadcrumbs, cheese, egg, parsley and nuts.
2 Preheat oven to 200°C/180°C fan-assisted.
3 Wash chicken under cold water; pat dry inside and out with absorbent paper. Tuck wing tips under chicken. Trim skin around neck; secure neck flap to underside of chicken with skewers.
4 Fill cavity with chorizo mixture, fold over skin to enclose stuffing; secure with cocktail sticks. Tie legs together with kitchen string. Place chicken and lemon in medium baking dish; rub chicken all over with remaining butter. Roast, uncovered, about 1½ hours or until chicken is cooked through, basting occasionally with pan juices. Remove and discard cocktail sticks.
5 Meanwhile, place ingredients for spinach and red onion salad in large bowl; toss gently to combine.

6 Serve chicken with stuffing, lemon and salad.

prep + cook time 2 hours
(+ cooling)
serves 4
nutritional count per serving
68.4g total fat (21.4g saturated fat); 967 cal (4042kJ); 24.4g carbohydrate; 60.3g protein; 5.8g fibre

CHICKEN WITH GARLIC POTATOES & ROSEMARY

8 x 200g chicken thighs
800g baby new potatoes, halved
30g butter, melted
2 rashers rindless bacon (130g), chopped coarsely
2 cloves garlic, sliced thinly
2 tablespoons fresh rosemary leaves
30g green olives

1 Preheat oven to 240°C/220°C fan-assisted. Cut two deep slashes through skin and flesh of the chicken to the bone.
2 Place chicken and potato in large, heavy-based flameproof baking dish. Brush with butter; roast, uncovered, 30 minutes.
3 Add bacon, garlic and rosemary to dish; roast, uncovered, further 10 minutes or until browned. Add olives.
4 Serve chicken and potato with a mixed salad and lemon wedges, if desired.

prep + cook time 50 minutes
serves 4
nutritional count per serving
50.8g total fat (18.8g saturated fat); 808 cal (3377kJ); 27.9g carbohydrate; 58.0g protein; 4.3g fibre

ROASTED POUSSINS WITH DILL & WALNUT PESTO & ORZO SALAD

4 tablespoons fresh flat-leaf parsley leaves

6 tablespoons fresh dill sprigs

50g roasted walnuts, chopped coarsely

20g finely grated parmesan cheese

60ml lemon juice

60ml olive oil

4 x 500g poussins

2 medium lemons (280g), quartered

orzo salad

220g orzo pasta

6 slices pancetta (90g), chopped finely

50g roasted pine nuts

3 tablespoons finely chopped fresh basil

3 tablespoons finely chopped fresh flat-leaf parsley

2 tablespoons olive oil

1 tablespoon red wine vinegar

1 Preheat oven to 180°C/160°C fan-assisted.

2 Blend or process herbs, nuts, cheese and juice until combined. With motor operating, gradually add oil in thin, steady stream until pesto thickens slightly. Reserve 1 tablespoon of pesto for orzo salad.

3 Wash poussins under cold water. Discard necks; pat dry inside and out with absorbent paper. Loosen poussin skin; rub remaining pesto between skin and flesh and over outside of poussins. Place 2 lemon quarters in cavity of each poussin.

4 Place poussins on oiled wire rack over baking dish; roast, uncovered, 45 minutes or until cooked through. Remove from dish; discard pan juices.

5 Meanwhile, make orzo salad.

6 Serve poussins, halved lengthways, on salad.

orzo salad cook pasta in large saucepan of boiling water, uncovered, until just tender; drain. Cook pancetta in heated oiled small frying pan, stirring, 5 minutes or until crisp. Place pasta and pancetta in large bowl with nuts, herbs, oil, vinegar and reserved pesto; toss gently to combine.

prep + cook time 1 hour 40 minutes

serves 4

nutritional count per serving 85.1g total fat (18.9g saturated fat); 1203 cal (5029kJ); 40.3g carbohydrate; 65.5g protein; 5.5g fibre

tip Orzo, sometimes called risoni, is pasta shaped like large grains of rice. If you can't find it, substitute other small pasta like trofie.

ROAST TURKEY WITH SAUSAGE STUFFING

4kg whole turkey
2 tablespoons olive oil
750ml chicken stock
40g butter
35g plain flour
60ml sweet sherry
sausage stuffing
1 tablespoon olive oil
1 small onion (80g), chopped
  finely
2 trimmed celery stalks (200g),
  chopped finely
2 rashers rindless bacon (130g),
  chopped finely
250g Italian pork sausages
280g stale breadcrumbs
2 teaspoons finely grated lemon
  rind
2 teaspoons lemon juice
2 tablespoons finely chopped
  fresh flat-leaf parsley
1 egg, beaten lightly

1 Make sausage stuffing. Preheat oven to 180°C/160°C fan-assisted.
2 Discard neck from turkey. Rinse turkey under cold running water; pat dry inside and out with absorbent paper. Fill neck cavity loosely with stuffing, secure skin over opening with cocktail sticks; fill large cavity loosely with stuffing. Tie legs with kitchen string; tuck wings under turkey.
3 Place turkey on oiled wire rack in large flameproof baking dish. Brush turkey with oil; add 250ml of the stock to dish. Cover with two layers of oiled foil; roast 2½ hours. Uncover; brush with pan juices. Roast, uncovered, 30 minutes or until browned all over and cooked through. Remove turkey from dish, cover; stand 20 minutes. Remove and discard cocktail sticks.
4 Drain pan juices from dish into large jug; skim and discard fat.
5 Melt butter in same dish over heat; cook flour, stirring, until mixture bubbles and thickens. Gradually add sherry, remaining stock and reserved pan juices; stir until it boils and thickens. Strain into same jug to serve.

sausage stuffing heat oil in medium frying pan; cook onion, celery and bacon, stirring, until onion softens. Squeeze sausage meat into large bowl; discard casings. Stir in onion mixture and remaining ingredients.

prep + cook time 3 hours 20 minutes (+ standing)
serves 8
nutritional count per serving 56.5g total fat (17.9g saturated fat); 913 cal (3816kJ); 29.4g carbohydrate; 69.7g protein; 2.3g fibre

tip Italian sausages are coarse pork sausages generally sold in plump links. They are usually flavoured with garlic and fennel seed or anise seed. Substitute any spicy pork sausages if you cannot obtain them.

ROAST GOOSE WITH FRUIT & NUT STUFFING

20g butter, melted
1 tablespoon honey
1 teaspoon light soy sauce
3.5kg whole goose
1 tablespoon plain flour
fruit & nut stuffing
2 tablespoons vegetable oil
200g chicken livers, chopped
   finely
1 medium onion (150g), chopped
   finely
1 trimmed celery stalk (100g),
   chopped finely
1 medium apple (150g), chopped
   finely
80g coarsely chopped brazil nuts
70g slivered almonds
75g coarsely chopped dried
   apricots
85g finely chopped raisins
1 tablespoon chopped fresh mint
   leaves
100g stale breadcrumbs

1 Preheat oven to 200°C/180°C
fan-assisted.
2 Make fruit & nut stuffing.
3 Combine butter, honey and
sauce in small bowl, brush mixture
inside and outside of goose.
Fill goose with stuffing, secure
opening with skewers. Tie legs
together, tuck wings under goose.
Prick skin to release fat during
roasting.
4 Lightly flour large oven bag;
place goose in bag, secure with
tie provided. Make holes in bag as
advised on package. Place goose
breast-side up in baking dish,
cover dish with foil; roast 1 hour.
Remove foil, roast goose further
1 hour. Remove and discard
skewers.
fruit & nut stuffing Heat half
the oil in medium saucepan;
cook chicken livers, stirring, until
browned; drain on absorbent
paper. Add remaining oil to pan;
cook onion and celery, stirring,
until onion is soft. Add apple and
nuts; cook, stirring, until nuts are
browned lightly. Remove from heat,
stir in livers, apricots, raisins, mint
and breadcrumbs; cool.

prep + cook time 3 hours
15 minutes
serves 8
nutritional count per serving
113.0g total fat (32.2g saturated
fat); 1293 cal (5405kJ); 27.0g
carbohydrate; 43.4g protein;
4.3g fibre

BEEF & VEAL

ROAST BEEF WITH YORKSHIRE PUDDINGS

2kg piece beef topside roast
500ml dry red wine
2 bay leaves
6 black peppercorns
70g wholegrain mustard
4 cloves garlic, sliced
4 sprigs fresh thyme
1 medium brown onion (150g), chopped coarsely
2 medium carrots (240g), chopped coarsely
1 large leek (500g), chopped coarsely
2 stalks celery (300g), trimmed, chopped coarsely
2 tablespoons olive oil
yorkshire puddings
150g plain flour
2 eggs
125ml milk
125ml water
gravy
2 tablespoons plain flour
375ml beef stock

1 Combine beef, wine, bay leaves, peppercorns, mustard, garlic, thyme and onion in large bowl, cover; refrigerate 3 hours or overnight.
2 Preheat oven to 180°C/160°C fan-assisted.
3 Drain beef over medium bowl; reserve 250ml of the marinade. Combine carrot, leek and celery in large baking dish, top with beef; brush beef with oil.
4 Roast beef, uncovered, about 1½ hours. Remove beef from dish, wrap in foil; stand 20 minutes before serving.
5 Increase oven temperature to 220°C/200°C fan-assisted.
6 Remove vegetables with slotted spoon; discard vegetables. Pour pan juices into jug; stand 2 minutes. Reserve 1½ tablespoons oil for yorkshire puddings, pour off excess oil; reserve 2 tablespoons of pan juices for gravy.
7 Make yorkshire puddings and gravy. Serve beef with yorkshire puddings and gravy; accompany with roasted potatoes and steamed baby carrots, if you like.

yorkshire puddings Sift flour into medium bowl; whisk in combined eggs, milk and water all at once until smooth. Stand batter 30 minutes. Divide the reserved oil among eight holes of 12-hole (80ml) muffin pan; heat in oven 2 minutes. Divide batter among pan holes. Bake about 20 minutes or until puddings are puffed and golden.

gravy Heat reserved pan juices in same baking dish, add flour; cook, stirring, until browned. Gradually add stock and reserved marinade; cook, stirring, until mixture boils and thickens. Strain gravy into heatproof jug.

prep + cook time 2 hours 35 minutes (+ refrigeration & standing)
serves 8
nutritional count per serving
15.4g total fat (4.8g saturated fat); 519 cal (2169kJ); 21.1g carbohydrate; 61.2g protein; 4g fibre

ROASTED BEEF FILLET WITH RÖSTI & CREAMED MUSHROOMS

2 tablespoons olive oil
800g beef fillet
1 large sweet potato (500g)
2 large waxy potatoes (600g)
80g butter
2 tablespoons olive oil, extra
30g butter, extra
200g chestnut mushrooms, halved
200g enoki mushrooms, trimmed
150g oyster mushrooms, halved
200g crème fraîche
3 spring onions, sliced thinly
4 tablespoons fresh flat-leaf parsley leaves

1 Preheat oven to 200°C/180°C fan-assisted.

2 Heat oil in large shallow flameproof baking dish; cook beef, uncovered, until browned all over. Roast, uncovered, in oven about 35 minutes or until cooked as desired. Cover to keep warm.

3 Meanwhile, coarsely grate sweet potato and potatoes into large bowl. Using hands, squeeze out excess moisture from potato mixture; shape mixture into eight portions. Heat 10g of the butter and 1 teaspoon of the extra oil in medium frying pan; spread one portion of the potato mixture over base of pan, flatten with spatula to form a firm pancake-like rösti. Cook, uncovered, over medium heat until browned; invert rösti onto large plate then gently slide back into pan to cook other side. Drain on absorbent paper; cover to keep warm. Repeat process with remaining butter, oil and potato mixture.

4 Heat extra butter in same cleaned pan; cook mushrooms, stirring, until just tender. Add crème fraîche; bring to the boil. Reduce heat; simmer, stirring, until sauce thickens slightly. Remove from heat; stir in onion and parsley.

5 Serve sliced beef with rösti and mushrooms.

prep + cook time 1 hour 5 minutes
serves 4
nutritional count per serving
69.9g total fat (34.1g saturated fat); 976 cal (4080kJ); 34.4g carbohydrate; 54.2g protein; 8.4g fibre

BEEF RIB ROAST WITH POTATO PURÉE & ROASTED BEETROOT

2kg beef standing rib roast
60ml olive oil
sea salt flakes
2 teaspoons cracked pepper
600g small beetroot, scrubbed, trimmed
1kg potatoes
40g butter, chopped
160ml milk, warmed
80ml double cream, warmed
3 tablespoons finely grated fresh horseradish

1 Preheat oven to 220°C/200°C fan-assisted.

2 Tie beef with kitchen string at 2cm intervals. Brush beef with 1 tablespoon of the oil; sprinkle with salt and pepper. Toss beetroot in remaining oil; add to dish. Roast, uncovered, about 20 minutes.

3 Reduce oven temperature to 180°C/160°C fan-assisted; roast beef and beetroot, uncovered, further 1 hour or until beef is cooked as desired. Remove beef from dish; cover, stand 20 minutes. Continue roasting the beetroot for a further 15 minutes or until it is tender.

4 Meanwhile, boil, steam or microwave potatoes until tender; drain. Mash potatoes; push through a sieve or mouli into a large bowl. Stir in butter then gradually beat in warmed milk and cream.

5 Serve beef with roast beetroot, potato purée and horseradish.

prep + cook time 2 hours (+ standing)
serves 4
nutritional count per serving
59.0g total fat (25.6g saturated fat); 1111 cal (4644kJ); 39.9g carbohydrate; 101.8g protein; 7.3g fibre

HERBED BEEF FILLET WITH HORSERADISH CREAM SAUCE

1 tablespoon finely grated lemon rind
80ml lemon juice
1 teaspoon dried chilli flakes
3 cloves garlic, crushed
3 tablespoons coarsely chopped fresh flat-leaf parsley
3 tablespoons fresh oregano leaves
3 tablespoons coarsely chopped fresh basil
3 tablespoons fresh marjoram leaves
80ml olive oil
2kg piece beef fillet
horseradish cream sauce
1 tablespoon olive oil
2 cloves garlic, crushed
2 teaspoons plain flour
125ml dry white wine
140g horseradish cream
600ml single cream

1 Preheat oven to 160°C/140°C fan-assisted.
2 Combine rind, juice, chilli, garlic, herbs and oil in large bowl. Coat beef all over with herb mixture. Place beef on oiled wire rack in large shallow baking dish. Roast, uncovered, about 40 minutes or until cooked as desired. Cover beef; stand 10 minutes.
3 Meanwhile, make horseradish cream sauce.
4 Serve sliced beef with sauce and beans, if desired.

horseradish cream sauce heat oil in small frying pan; cook garlic and flour, stirring, until mixture bubbles and browns lightly. Gradually stir in wine; bring to the boil, stirring. Reduce heat; simmer, uncovered, until liquid reduces by half. Stir in horseradish and cream; simmer, stirring, about 5 minutes or until sauce thickens slightly.

prep + cook time 55 minutes (+ standing)
serves 8
nutritional count per serving
60.5g total fat (30.4g saturated fat); 794 cal (3319kJ); 5.7g carbohydrate; 55.2g protein; 0.8g fibre

MEDITERRANEAN ROAST BEEF & VEGETABLES

1.5kg piece beef silverside
80ml olive oil
6 whole baby onions (150g)
3 medium courgettes (360g),
   halved lengthways
6 medium plum tomatoes (450g),
   halved
3 finger aubergines (180g), halved
   lengthways
2 medium yellow peppers (400g),
   quartered
2 tablespoons balsamic vinegar
2 tablespoons shredded fresh
   basil
2 tablespoons chopped fresh
   tarragon
1 tablespoon drained baby capers

1 Preheat oven to 200°C/180°C
fan-assisted.
2 Rub beef with 2 teaspoons
of the oil; sprinkle with salt and
freshly ground black pepper.
Heat 1 tablespoon of the oil in
flameproof baking dish; cook
beef until browned all over. Add
onions to dish; roast, uncovered,
in oven 20 minutes.
3 Place courgettes, tomato,
aubergine and pepper around
beef in dish; roast further
40 minutes or until beef is cooked
as desired. Remove beef from
dish, cover with foil; stand
10 minutes.
4 Increase oven temperature to
240°C/220°C fan-assisted; roast
vegetables further 10 minutes
or until browned and tender.
Drizzle vegetables with combined
remaining oil, vinegar, herbs and
baby capers.
5 Serve thinly sliced beef with
vegetable mixture.

prep + cook time 1 hour
35 minutes (+ standing)
serves 6
nutritional count per serving
24.6g total fat (7.0g saturated
fat); 480 cal (2006kJ); 5.6g
carbohydrate; 57.5g protein;
3.3g fibre
tip If you can't find small finger
aubergines use a large aubergine
sliced lengthways.

VEAL RACK WITH ROASTED MUSHROOM SAUCE

1kg veal rack
60ml olive oil
sea salt flakes
1kg baby new potatoes
300g button mushrooms
150g shimeji or oyster
   mushrooms
2 cloves garlic, sliced
2 tablespoons grated parmesan
   cheese
2 tablespoons plain flour
375ml chicken stock
80ml double cream
2 tablespoons chopped fresh
   flat-leaf parsley

1 Preheat oven to 200°C/180°C fan-assisted.

2 Place veal on oiled wire rack in shallow flameproof medium baking dish. Rub veal with 1 tablespoon of the oil, sprinkle with sea salt flakes and freshly ground black pepper; roast for 10 minutes.

3 Place potatoes in separate small baking dish; roast potatoes alongside veal for further 30 minutes or until veal is cooked as desired, brushing with any pan juices. Remove veal from dish; cover to keep warm.

4 Combine mushrooms, garlic and remaining oil in dish used to bake veal; roast mushroom mixture alongside potatoes for further 20 minutes or until potatoes are tender. Sprinkle potatoes with cheese, then roast a further 5 minutes or until cheese is melted.

5 Meanwhile, place baking dish containing mushroom mixture over medium heat, add flour; cook, stirring, about 2 minutes or until bubbling. Gradually stir in stock and any juices that have run from the veal; cook, stirring, until sauce boils and thickens. Stir in cream and parsley until heated through.

6 Cut the veal into cutlets, serve with mushroom sauce and potatoes.

prep + cook time 1 hour 25 minutes
serves 4
nutritional count per serving 29.0g total fat (10.0g saturated fat); 668 cal (2792kJ); 38.7g carbohydrate; 58.4g protein; 9.1g fibre

ANCHOVY & GARLIC VEAL WITH ROASTED FENNEL

3 drained anchovy fillets
4 cloves garlic, chopped coarsely
3 teaspoons fresh rosemary
  leaves
1 teaspoon salt
1 teaspoon cracked black pepper
1 tablespoon olive oil
1kg rack of veal (8 cutlets)
2 medium red onions (340g),
  sliced thickly
2 bay leaves
8 baby fennel bulbs (1kg),
  trimmed, halved or quartered
125ml dry white wine
250ml chicken stock
12 small vine tomatoes (350g)

1 Preheat oven to 200°C/180°C fan-assisted.
2 Using mortar and pestle or small blender, pound anchovies, garlic, rosemary, salt and pepper until mixture forms a paste; stir in oil. Rub anchovy mixture over veal. Cover; refrigerate for 1 hour.
3 Place onion and bay leaves in baking dish; place veal on top of onion. Place fennel around veal, add wine and stock; roast, uncovered, about 40 minutes or until veal is cooked as desired. Add extra stock if pan juices evaporate. Remove veal; cover to keep warm.
4 Meanwhile, add tomatoes to baking dish; roast, uncovered, with fennel for further 15 minutes or until softened slightly. Discard bay leaves.
5 Serve veal with vegetables and pan juices.

prep + cook time 1 hour 15 minutes (+ refrigeration)
serves 4
nutritional count per serving
10.1g total fat (2.3g saturated fat); 372 cal (1555kJ); 11.6g carbohydrate; 50.1g protein; 6.7g fibre

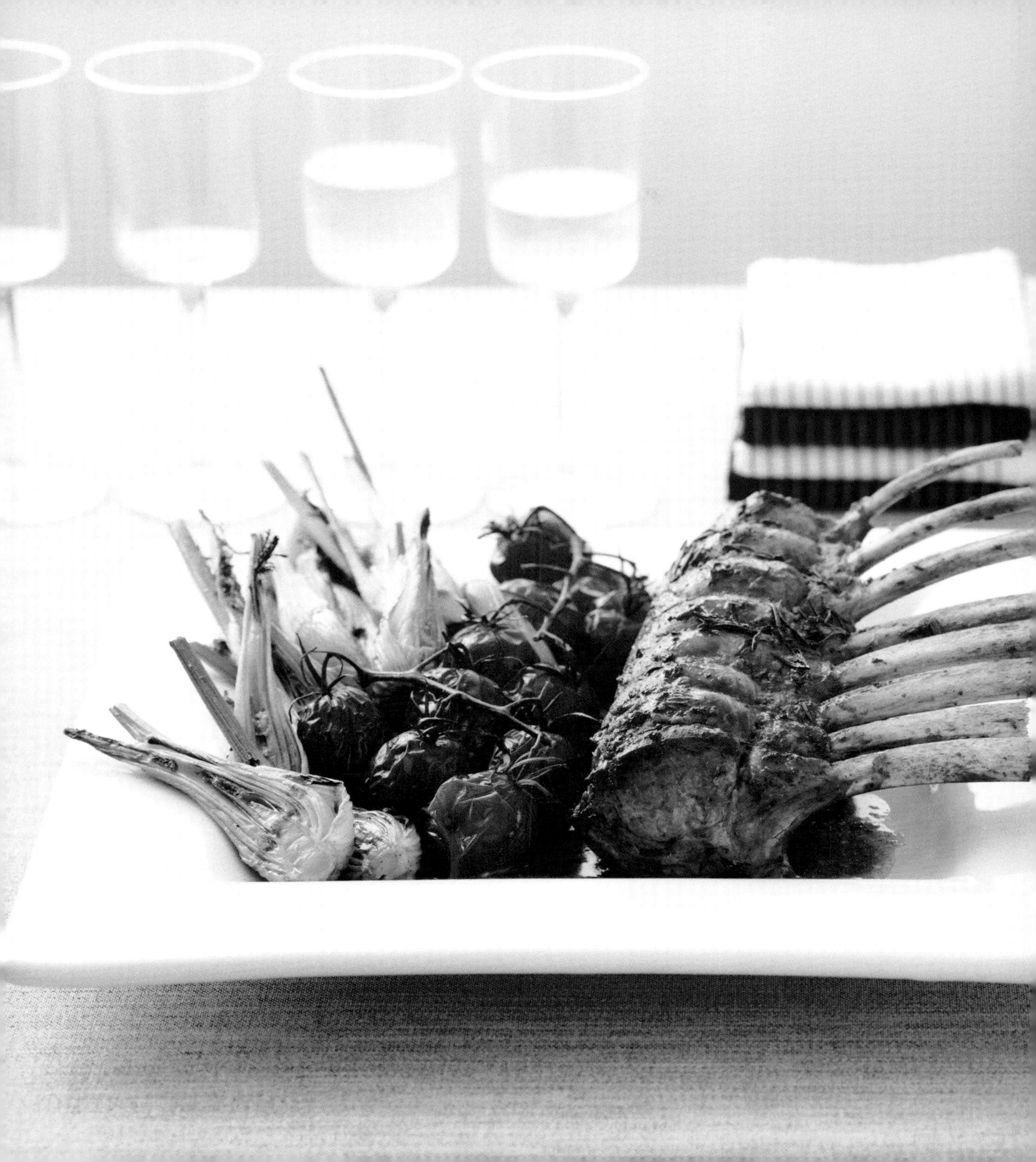

MUSTARD-CRUSTED RACK OF VEAL WITH SWEET POTATO MASH

2 tablespoons wholegrain mustard

3 spring onions, chopped finely

2 cloves garlic, crushed

1 tablespoon finely chopped fresh rosemary

2 tablespoons olive oil

1kg veal rack (8 cutlets), trimmed

2 small sweet potatoes (500g), chopped coarsely

20g butter

80ml double cream

1 large brown onion (200g), sliced thinly

400g mushrooms, sliced thinly

1 tablespoon plain flour

60ml dry white wine

180ml chicken stock

3 tablespoons coarsely chopped fresh flat-leaf parsley

1 Preheat oven to 200°C/180°C fan-assisted.

2 Combine mustard, spring onion, half of the garlic, rosemary and half of the oil in small jug. Place veal on oiled wire rack over large shallow flameproof baking dish; coat veal all over with mustard mixture. Roast, uncovered, about 30 minutes or until browned all over and cooked as desired. Cover to keep warm.

3 Meanwhile, boil, steam or microwave sweet potatoes until tender; drain. Mash sweet potato in large bowl with butter and half of the cream until smooth.

4 Heat remaining oil in same flameproof dish; cook brown onion and remaining garlic, stirring, until onion softens. Add mushrooms; cook, stirring, about 5 minutes or until just tender. Add flour; cook, stirring, until mixture bubbles and thickens. Gradually stir in wine and stock; stir until sauce boils and thickens. Add remaining cream and parsley; stir until heated through.

5 Serve veal with sweet potato mash and mushroom sauce.

prep + cook time 1 hour
serves 4
nutritional count per serving
27.4g total fat (11.2g saturated fat); 567 cal (2370kJ); 21.8g carbohydrate; 53.2g protein; 6.0g fibre

LAMB

SPRING ROAST LAMB WITH MINT SAUCE

2 tablespoons olive oil
4 cloves garlic, crushed
2 tablespoons lemon juice
2 tablespoons fresh oregano
   leaves
2kg boned leg lamb
1kg desiree potatoes, cut into
   wedges
250ml chicken stock
2 sprigs fresh rosemary
mint sauce
3 good handfuls fresh mint leaves
2 tablespoons ground almonds
2 cloves garlic, quartered
80ml olive oil
2 tablespoons lemon juice

1 Combine oil, garlic, juice and oregano in small bowl. Rub lamb all over with garlic mixture, inside and out. Cover; refrigerate 3 hours or overnight.
2 Preheat oven to 200°C/180°C fan-assisted.
3 Place potatoes in large oiled baking dish. Pour stock over potatoes; top with rosemary sprigs. Place lamb on top of potatoes. Roast, uncovered, about 1 hour or until lamb is cooked as desired. Remove lamb from dish; cover, stand 15 minutes.
4 Increase oven temperature to 240°C/230°C fan-assisted; roast potatoes further 15 minutes or until browned.
5 Make mint sauce.
6 Serve lamb with potatoes and sauce, and red coleslaw, if desired.
mint sauce Blend or process mint, ground almonds and garlic until finely chopped. Transfer mixture to small bowl; stir in oil and lemon juice.

prep + cook time 1 hour 35 minutes (+ refrigeration)
serves 6
nutritional count per serving 38.4g total fat (10.8g saturated fat); 745 cal (3114kJ); 19.3g carbohydrate; 78.7g protein; 4.1g fibre

CRUSTED LAMB RACKS & POTATO WEDGES

5 medium potatoes (1kg), cut into wedges
60ml olive oil
4 x 4 french-trimmed cutlet lamb racks (600g)
½ teaspoon dried chilli flakes
2 tablespoons kalonji seeds
2 tablespoons sesame seeds
1 clove garlic, crushed
2 handfuls fresh flat-leaf parsley leaves

1 Preheat oven to 200°C/180°C fan-assisted.
2 Combine potato wedges with 2 tablespoons of the oil on oven tray. Roast potato, in single layer, uncovered, about 55 minutes or until browned lightly and crisp.
3 Meanwhile, place lamb on separate oven tray; rub all over with combined remaining oil, chilli, seeds and garlic. Roast, uncovered, for last 20 minutes of potato cooking time or until lamb is browned and cooked as desired.
4 Combine potatoes and parsley in large bowl; serve with lamb and lemon, if desired.

prep + cook time 1 hour 10 minutes
serves 4
nutritional count per serving
31.6g total fat (8.4g saturated fat); 489 cal (2044kJ); 28.9g carbohydrate; 22.4g protein; 4.8g fibre

PORT & BALSAMIC SLOW-ROASTED LAMB

2.5kg leg of lamb
30g sea salt flakes
20g butter
1 tablespoon olive oil
80ml dry red wine
80ml balsamic vinegar
80ml port
60ml beef stock
8 cloves garlic, crushed
8 medium plum tomatoes (600g),
   halved lengthways

1 Preheat oven to 120°C/100°C fan-assisted.
2 Bring a large saucepan of water to the boil; add lamb, simmer 15 minutes. Drain; pat lamb dry. Using sharp knife, pierce lamb all over; press salt into cuts.
3 Heat butter and oil in large flameproof dish; cook lamb, turning, until browned all over. Add wine, vinegar, port, stock and garlic to dish; roast lamb, covered, in oven 4½ hours.
4 Add tomatoes, cut-side up, to dish; roast further 2 hours, uncovered, basting occasionally.
5 Remove lamb and tomatoes from dish; boil pan juices over heat until reduced by half. Serve with lamb and tomatoes.

prep + cook time 7 hours 10 minutes
serves 6
nutritional count per serving
22.7g total fat (9.7g saturated fat); 522 cal (2186kJ); 4.5g carbohydrate; 69.6g protein; 2.1g fibre

TRADITIONAL ROAST LAMB DINNER

2kg leg of lamb
3 sprigs fresh rosemary, chopped
  coarsely
½ teaspoon sweet paprika
1kg potatoes, chopped coarsely
500g piece pumpkin (or butternut
  squash), chopped coarsely
3 small onions (240g), halved
2 tablespoons olive oil
2 tablespoons plain flour
250ml chicken stock
60ml dry red wine

1 Preheat oven to 200°C/180°C fan-assisted.
2 Place lamb in large oiled baking dish; using sharp knife, score skin at 2cm intervals, sprinkle with rosemary and paprika. Roast, uncovered, 15 minutes. Reduce oven temperature to 180°C/160°C fan-assisted; roast, uncovered, further 45 minutes or until cooked as desired.
3 Meanwhile, place potato, pumpkin and onion, in single layer, in large shallow baking dish; drizzle with oil. Roast, uncovered, alongside lamb for last 45 minutes of lamb cooking time. Remove lamb and vegetables from oven; cover to keep warm.
4 Strain pan juices from lamb dish into medium jug. Return 60ml of the pan juices to flameproof dish over medium heat, add flour; cook, stirring, 5 minutes or until mixture bubbles and browns. Gradually stir in stock and wine; cook over high heat, stirring, until gravy boils and thickens. Strain.
5 Serve sliced lamb with roasted vegetables and gravy and, if desired, cauliflower cheese.

prep + cook time 1 hour 40 minutes
serves 6
nutritional count per serving
20.1g total fat (7.1g saturated fat); 554 cal (2316kJ); 28.5g carbohydrate; 60.9g protein; 3.8g fibre

LAMB BRETONNE

1.5kg leg of lamb
1 clove garlic, sliced thinly
2 sprigs fresh rosemary
1 teaspoon sea salt flakes
½ teaspoon freshly cracked black pepper
20g butter
2 medium brown onions (300g), sliced thinly
3 cloves garlic, crushed
400g can chopped tomatoes
410g passata
500ml beef stock
400g can cannellini or butter beans, rinsed, drained

1 Preheat oven to 180°C/160°C fan-assisted.
2 Trim excess fat from lamb. Pierce lamb in several places with sharp knife; press sliced garlic and a little of the rosemary firmly into cuts. Rub salt and pepper over lamb.
3 Heat butter in large flameproof baking dish on cooker top; cook onion and crushed garlic, stirring, until onion browns slightly. Stir in undrained tomatoes, passata, stock, beans and remaining rosemary; bring to the boil then remove from heat.
4 Place lamb, pierced-side down, on bean mixture; cover. Transfer dish to oven; cook 1 hour. Uncover, turn lamb carefully; cook, brushing occasionally with tomato mixture, about 1 hour or until lamb is cooked.

prep & cook time 2 hours 30 minutes
serves 4
nutritional count per serving
19.9g total fat (9.5g saturated fat); 556 cal (2324kJ); 20.2g carbohydrate; 69.8g protein; 7.7g fibre

LAMB SHANKS IN FIVE-SPICE, TAMARIND & GINGER

2 teaspoons five-spice powder
1 teaspoon dried chilli flakes
1 cinnamon stick
2 star anise
60ml soy sauce
125ml chinese cooking wine
2 tablespoons tamarind
    concentrate
2 tablespoons brown sugar
8cm piece fresh ginger (40g),
    grated
2 cloves garlic, chopped coarsely
310ml water
8 french-trimmed lamb shanks
    (1.6kg)
500g choy sum or bok choy, cut
    into 10cm lengths
150g sugar snap peas, trimmed

1 Preheat oven to 180°C/160°C fan-assisted.
2 Dry-fry five-spice, chilli, cinnamon and star anise in small frying pan, stirring, until fragrant. Combine spices with soy sauce, wine, tamarind, sugar, ginger, garlic and the water in medium jug.
3 Place shanks, in single layer, in large shallow baking dish; drizzle with spice mixture. Roast, uncovered, turning shanks occasionally, about 2 hours or until meat is almost falling off the bone. Remove shanks from dish; cover to keep warm. Skim away excess fat from pan juices; strain sauce into small saucepan.
4 Meanwhile, boil, steam or microwave choy sum and peas, separately, until tender; drain.
5 Divide vegetables among serving plates; serve with shanks, drizzled with reheated sauce.

prep + cook time 2 hours 30 minutes
serves 4
nutritional count per serving
20.0g total fat (9.0g saturated fat); 451 cal (1885kJ); 12.5g carbohydrate; 48.3g protein; 3.1g fibre

GREEK ROAST LAMB WITH SKORDALIA & POTATOES

2kg leg of lamb
2 cloves garlic, crushed
125ml lemon juice
2 tablespoons olive oil
1 tablespoon fresh oregano
  leaves
1 teaspoon fresh lemon thyme
  leaves
5 large potatoes (1.5kg), cut into
  3cm cubes
1 tablespoon finely grated lemon
  rind
2 tablespoons lemon juice, extra
2 tablespoons olive oil, extra
1 teaspoon fresh lemon thyme
  leaves, extra

skordalia
1 medium potato (200g),
  quartered
3 cloves garlic, crushed
1 tablespoon lemon juice
1 tablespoon white wine vinegar
2 tablespoons water
80ml olive oil

1 Combine lamb with garlic, juice, oil, oregano and thyme in large bowl. Cover; refrigerate 3 hours or overnight.
2 Preheat oven to 160°C/140°C fan-assisted.
3 Place lamb in large baking dish; roast, uncovered, 4 hours.
4 Meanwhile, make skordalia.
5 Combine potatoes in large bowl with rind and extra juice, oil and thyme. Place potatoes, in single layer, on oven tray. Roast potatoes for last 30 minutes of lamb cooking time.
6 Remove lamb from oven; cover to keep warm.
7 Increase oven temperature to 220°C/200°C fan-assisted; roast potatoes a further 20 minutes or until browned lightly and cooked through. Serve potatoes and lamb with skordalia.

skordalia Boil, steam or microwave potato until tender; drain. Push potato through food mill or fine sieve into medium bowl; cool 10 minutes. Whisk combined garlic, juice, vinegar and the water into potato. Gradually whisk in oil in a thin, steady stream; continue whisking until skordalia thickens. Stir in about a tablespoon of warm water if skordalia is too thick. Serve sprinkled with extra lemon thyme leaves, if you like.

prep + cook time 4 hours
50 minutes (+ refrigeration)
serves 4
nutritional count per serving
57g total fat (14g saturated fat); 1090 cal (4556kJ); 51.5g carbohydrate; 91.2g protein; 6.7g fibre

ROASTED SPICED LAMB & VEGETABLES

2 x 350g mini lamb roasts
1 tablespoon olive oil
250g cherry tomatoes
2 medium courgettes (240g),
    halved lengthways
250g baby red peppers or 1 large
    red pepper (350g), quartered
spice rub
2 tablespoons olive oil
1 teaspoon dried oregano leaves
3 cloves garlic, crushed
¼ teaspoon salt
1 teaspoon sweet paprika
1 tablespoon lemon juice

1 Preheat oven to 240°C/220°C
fan-assisted.
2 Combine ingredients for spice
rub in small bowl; rub half of the
spice rub over lamb.
3 Heat oil in medium flameproof
baking dish; cook lamb, over heat,
until browned all over. Roast,
uncovered, in oven for 10 minutes.
4 Combine remaining spice rub
with vegetables in medium baking
dish; roast alongside lamb
15 minutes. Remove lamb; cover,
stand 10 minutes.
5 Roast vegetables further
5 minutes or until tender.
6 Serve lamb with vegetables.

prep + cook time 50 minutes
serves 4
nutritional count per serving
29.5g total fat (8.9g saturated
fat); 443 cal (1852kJ); 4.9g
carbohydrate; 38.7g protein;
3.1g fibre

LAMB WITH AÏOLI

80ml olive oil
6 sprigs fresh thyme
900g large potatoes
6 x 4 french-trimmed cutlet lamb
   racks (900g)
500g spinach, trimmed
20g butter
1 clove garlic, crushed
250g chestnut mushrooms, sliced
   thickly
1 tablespoon balsamic vinegar
aïoli
½ teaspoon dijon mustard
1 tablespoon white wine vinegar
1 clove garlic, crushed
2 egg yolks
180ml extra virgin olive oil
2 teaspoons lemon juice

1 Heat oil in small saucepan;
deep-fry thyme briefly, about
5 seconds or until fragrant.
Remove thyme from oil, drain on
absorbent paper; reserve oil.
2 Preheat oven to 200°C/180°C
fan-assisted.
3 Cut potatoes into 1cm slices.
Heat 2 tablespoons of the
reserved thyme oil in flameproof
baking dish; cook potato slices, in
batches, until lightly browned both
sides. Return all potato to same
baking dish.
4 Add lamb to baking dish;
roast, uncovered, in oven about
15 minutes or until cooked as
desired. Cover to keep warm.
5 Meanwhile, make aïoli.
6 Boil, steam or microwave
spinach until just wilted; drain.
7 Heat remaining thyme oil with
butter in small saucepan; cook
garlic and mushrooms, stirring,
until mushrooms soften.
8 Cut lamb racks into cutlets;
divide among serving plates with
spinach, potato and mushrooms.
Top with aïoli, garnish with fried
thyme; drizzle with vinegar.

aïoli Whisk mustard, vinegar,
garlic and egg yolks in small bowl
until combined. Gradually add oil
in thin, steady stream, whisking
constantly, until aïoli thickens.
Whisk in lemon juice.

prep + cook time 1 hour
5 minutes
serves 6
nutritional count per serving
51.4g total fat (11.3g saturated
fat); 646 cal (2700kJ); 20.2g
carbohydrate; 24.2g protein;
5.4g fibre

MARINATED LAMB LEG WITH CAPONATA

2kg leg of lamb
2 teaspoons sweet paprika
60ml lemon juice
1 tablespoon olive oil
2 cloves garlic, crushed
750ml beef stock
2 teaspoons finely shredded
   lemon rind
2 tablespoons coarsely chopped
   fresh lemon thyme
caponata
2 tablespoons olive oil
6 baby aubergines (360g),
   chopped coarsely
2 medium brown onions (300g),
   chopped coarsely
3 cloves garlic, crushed
2 trimmed celery stalks (200g),
   chopped coarsely
2 medium red peppers (400g),
   chopped coarsely
1 tablespoon drained baby
   capers, rinsed
2 tablespoons red wine vinegar
3 large plum tomatoes (270g),
   chopped coarsely
6 tablespoons coarsely chopped
   fresh basil
40g roasted pine nuts

1 Using sharp knife, pierce lamb all over; rub combined paprika, juice, oil and garlic over lamb, pressing into cuts. Cover; refrigerate 3 hours or overnight.
2 Preheat oven to 200°C/180°C fan-assisted. Pour stock into large shallow baking dish; place lamb on oiled rack over dish, drizzle any remaining paprika mixture. Roast, uncovered, 30 minutes, brushing occasionally with pan juices. Reduce oven temperature to 180°C/160°C fan-assisted; roast, uncovered, 1¼ hours or until lamb is cooked as desired. Cover lamb; stand 20 minutes.
3 Meanwhile, make caponata. Serve sliced lamb, sprinkled with combined rind and thyme, with caponata and, if desired, soft polenta.

caponata Heat half of the oil in large saucepan; cook aubergine until browned. Remove from pan. Heat remaining oil in same pan; cook onion, stirring, until soft. Add garlic, celery and pepper; cook, stirring, until vegetables soften. Stir in capers, vinegar, tomato, aubergine and half of the basil; cook, covered, over low heat about 15 minutes or until mixture thickens slightly. Stir in remaining basil and pine nuts just before serving.

prep + cook time 2 hours 15 minutes (+ refrigeration and standing)
serves 4
nutritional count per serving
41.8g total fat (11.4g saturated fat); 810 cal (3386kJ); 14.9g carbohydrate; 90.2g protein; 7.3g fibre

PORK

ROAST ROLLED PORK LOIN & CRACKLING

2.5kg boneless loin of pork,
  rind on
1 tablespoon olive oil
2 teaspoons fine sea salt
1 tablespoon plain flour
375ml chicken stock
apricot, prune & rice stuffing
130g white long-grain rice
75g finely chopped dried apricots
105g finely chopped prunes

1 Preheat oven to 240°C/220°C fan-assisted.
2 Place pork on board, rind-side up. Run a sharp knife about 5mm under rind, between it and the meat, gradually lifting and easing rind away from pork. Place rind, right-side up, in large shallow flameproof baking dish. Score rind, making diagonal cuts; rub with half of the oil, sprinkle with salt. Roast, uncovered, about 40 minutes or until crackling is well browned and crisp. Chop crackling into serving pieces. Reduce oven temperature to 220°C/200°C fan-assisted.
3 Meanwhile, make apricot, prune and rice stuffing.
4 Place pork, fat-side down, on board. Slice through the thickest part of the meat horizontally, without cutting through at the side. Open out meat to form one large piece; press stuffing against the loin along width. Roll pork to enclose stuffing; secure with kitchen string at 2cm intervals.
5 Return pork to same dish, brush with remaining oil; roast, uncovered, 1 hour or until cooked through. Remove from dish; cover to keep warm.

6 Pour pan juices from pork dish into medium jug. Add 1 tablespoon of the pan juices to pork dish over medium heat, stir in flour; cook, stirring, until mixture bubbles and is browned to your liking. Gradually add remaining pan juices and stock; cook, stirring, until gravy boils and thickens. Pour gravy into serving jug.
7 Serve pork with gravy and reheated crackling.
apricot, prune & rice stuffing
Cook rice in large saucepan of boiling water, uncovered, 15 minutes or until just tender; drain. Combine cooled rice in large bowl with remaining ingredients.

prep + cook time 2 hours 30 minutes (+ cooling)
serves 6
nutritional count per serving
96.4g total fat (32.2g saturated fat); 1298 cal (5426kJ); 29.8g carbohydrate; 78.7g protein; 2.7g fibre
tip If you prefer, ask your butcher to remove the rind completely from the pork loin and score it for you.

POT ROAST PORK WITH APPLE & SAGE

1.5kg piece pork neck
1 tablespoon olive oil
600g spring onions, stems
  trimmed to 10cm lengths
6 large sprigs fresh sage
6 large sprigs fresh thyme
250ml dry white wine
2 tablespoons boiling water
40g butter
3 large apples (600g), unpeeled,
  cored, cut into thick wedges

1 Cook pork with 2 teaspoons of the oil in heated large heavy-based saucepan, turning, until browned all over. Add onions, herbs and wine to pan; bring to the boil. Reduce heat; simmer, covered tightly, about 1½ hours or until pork is cooked, turning pork twice during cooking time. Transfer pork and onions to serving platter; cover to keep warm.

2 Strain pan juices into serving jug; discard solids. Stir the water into jug; cover to keep sauce warm.

3 Meanwhile, heat butter and remaining oil in large frying pan; cook apple, stirring, about 10 minutes or until tender and golden.

4 Serve sliced pork with sauce, apple and onions and, if you like, mashed or roasted potatoes.

prep + cook time 2 hours
serves 6
nutritional count per serving
28.8g total fat (16.8g saturated fat); 572 cal (2391kJ); 14.7g carbohydrate; 55.1g protein; 3.8g fibre
tip Granny Smith or Golden Delicious apples are best for this recipe.

SLOW-ROASTED HONEY & SOY PORK NECK

1 tablespoon groundnut oil
1kg piece pork neck
1 large brown onion (200g),
  sliced thinly
2 cloves garlic, sliced thinly
4cm piece fresh ginger (20g),
  sliced thinly
1 cinnamon stick
2 star anise
125ml soy sauce
125ml chinese cooking wine
90g honey
250ml water
450g baby bok choy, trimmed,
  leaves separated

1 Preheat oven to 160°C/140°C fan-assisted.
2 Heat oil in large flameproof casserole dish; cook pork, turning occasionally, until browned. Remove from dish. Add onion, garlic and ginger to same heated dish; cook, stirring, until onion softens. Remove from heat.
3 Stir cinnamon, star anise, sauce, cooking wine, honey and the water into onion mixture in dish. Return pork to dish, turning to coat in spice mixture.
4 Cover dish; transfer to oven. Cook 1 hour. Uncover; cook about 1 hour or until sauce thickens slightly. Remove pork from dish. Cover pork; stand 10 minutes before slicing.
5 Add bok choy to dish; cook, stirring, over medium heat on cooker top, about 5 minutes or until just tender. Serve pork with bok choy and sauce.

prep + cook time 2 hours 35 minutes
serves 4
nutritional count per serving
30.6g total fat (9.8g saturated fat); 627 cal (2621kJ); 5.9g carbohydrate; 76.4g protein; 2.5g fibre

PORK LOIN WITH PRUNES, POTATOES & PEARS

70g stale multigrain breadcrumbs

3 cloves garlic, crushed

1 tablespoon coarsely chopped fresh sage

40g pitted prunes, chopped coarsely

45g finely chopped dried figs

2 tablespoons greek-style yogurt

1.7kg lean pork loin

1 tablespoon lemon juice

1 tablespoon coarse cooking salt

2 medium brown onions (300g), cut into wedges

3 small firm pears (440g), quartered

1kg salad potatoes, halved lengthways

2 tablespoons olive oil

1 Preheat the oven to 240°C/ 220°C fan-assisted.

2 Combine breadcrumbs, garlic, sage, prunes, figs and yogurt in small bowl. Place mixture against the pork loin along the length. Roll pork to enclose seasoning; secure with kitchen string at 2cm intervals.

3 Place pork on oiled wire rack in medium baking dish; rub with combined juice and salt. Roast, uncovered, about 20 minutes or until skin blisters. Drain fat from dish. Reduce oven temperature to 180°C/160°C fan-assisted; add onion and pear to dish, roast, uncovered, 20 minutes.

4 Place combined potatoes and oil in separate medium baking dish; roast, uncovered, 50 minutes or until pork is cooked through and potatoes are tender.

5 Serve pork with onion, pears and potatoes.

prep + cook time 1 hour 50 minutes

serves 6

nutritional count per serving 70.6g total fat (22.8g saturated fat); 1065 cal (4452kJ); 46.3g carbohydrate; 58.7g protein; 8.1g fibre

ROAST PORK WITH GARLIC & ROSEMARY

1.5kg neck of pork
3 cloves garlic, crushed
1 tablespoon chopped fresh
  rosemary
1 tablespoon coarse cooking salt
2 tablespoons olive oil
3 bay leaves
250ml water
80ml red wine vinegar

1 Preheat oven to 200°C/180°C fan-assisted.
2 Tie pork with kitchen string at 3cm intervals.
3 Combine garlic, rosemary, salt and oil in small bowl; rub mixture over pork. Place pork on wire rack in baking dish; add bay leaves, the water and vinegar to dish.
4 Roast pork about 1½ hours or until cooked through. Cover pork; stand 10 minutes before slicing.

prep + cook time 1 hour 50 minutes (+ standing)
serves 6
nutritional count per serving
26.1g total fat (7.6g saturated fat); 449 cal (1877kJ); 0.2g carbohydrate; 53.1g protein; 0.3g fibre

HONEY-GLAZED PORK WITH SAGE

2.5kg boneless loin of pork
2 teaspoons vegetable oil
1 tablespoon fine sea salt
2 cloves garlic, crushed
1 tablespoon finely chopped fresh
  sage
90g honey, warmed
1 tablespoon red wine vinegar
500ml chicken stock
2 tablespoons cornflour
2 tablespoons water

1 Preheat oven to 240°C/220°C fan-assisted.
2 Place pork on board, rind-side up. Run a sharp knife about 5mm under rind, between it and the meat, gradually lifting and easing rind away from pork. Place rind, right-side up, in large shallow flameproof baking dish. Score rind, making diagonal cuts; rub with the oil and salt. Roast, uncovered, about 40 minutes or until crackling is well browned and crisp; cool. Discard fat from baking dish.
3 Place pork, fat-side down, on board; sprinkle with half of the garlic and half of the sage. Roll pork to enclose sage and garlic; secure with kitchen string at 2cm intervals. Place pork on wire rack in same baking dish.
4 Reduce oven temperature to 200°C/180°C fan-assisted; roast pork, uncovered, 30 minutes. Cover with foil; reduce oven temperature to 180°C/160°C fan-assisted. Roast 1 hour.
5 Combine honey, vinegar and remaining sage and garlic in small bowl. Remove foil from pork, brush pork with half of the honey mixture. Roast, uncovered,

30 minutes or until browned and cooked through, brushing occasionally with remaining honey mixture. Remove pork from dish; cover with foil.
6 Strain pan juices from baking dish into heatproof jug; remove fat from pan juices (you will need 165ml of pan juices). Add stock to baking dish; stir in combined cornflour and water over heat until sauce boils and thickens. Serve pork slices with sauce and crackling.

prep + cook time 3 hours
serves 8
nutritional count per serving
71.1g total fat (24.0g saturated fat); 910 cal (3804kJ); 12.0g carbohydrate; 57.3g protein; 0.1g fibre

tip If you prefer, ask your butcher to remove the rind completely from the pork loin and score it for you.

PORK LOIN WITH SPINACH & PANCETTA STUFFING

4 slices white bread (120g)
2 tablespoons olive oil
1 clove garlic, crushed
1 medium brown onion (150g), chopped coarsely
6 slices pancetta (90g), chopped coarsely
100g baby spinach leaves
35g roasted macadamias, chopped coarsely
125ml chicken stock
2kg boneless pork loin
plum & red wine sauce
480g plum jam
2 tablespoons dry red wine
160ml chicken stock

1 Preheat oven to 200°C/180°C fan-assisted.
2 Remove and discard bread crusts; cut bread into 1cm cubes. Heat half of the oil in large frying pan; cook bread, stirring, until browned and crisp. Drain croutons on absorbent paper.
3 Heat remaining oil in same pan; cook garlic, onion and pancetta until onion browns lightly. Stir in spinach; remove from heat. Gently stir in croutons, nuts and stock.
4 Place pork on board, fat-side down; slice through thickest part of pork horizontally, without cutting through other side. Open out pork to form one large piece; press stuffing mixture against loin along width of pork. Roll pork to enclose stuffing, securing with kitchen string at 2cm intervals.
5 Place rolled pork on rack in large shallow baking dish. Roast, uncovered, 1¼ hours or until cooked through.
6 Meanwhile, make plum and red wine sauce; serve with sliced pork.

plum & red wine sauce Bring ingredients to the boil in small saucepan. Reduce heat; simmer, uncovered, 10 minutes or until sauce thickens slightly.

prep + cook time 2 hours
serves 10
nutritional count per serving 25.7g total fat (7.1g saturated fat); 588 cal (2458kJ); 40.3g carbohydrate; 47.0g protein; 1.8g fibre

PORK LOIN WITH COUSCOUS & APPLES

200g couscous
250ml boiling water
55g pitted prunes, chopped finely
1 tablespoon roasted pine nuts
2 tablespoons coarsely chopped
  fresh coriander
3 tablespoons coarsely chopped
  fresh flat-leaf parsley
500g boneless pork loin, rind off
625ml cider
2 medium apples (300g), peeled,
  cored, sliced thickly
1 large red onion (300g), cut into
  thick wedges
2 tablespoons brown sugar

1 Preheat oven to 200°C/180°C fan-assisted.
2 Combine couscous with the water in medium heatproof bowl. Cover; stand 5 minutes or until water is absorbed, fluffing with fork occasionally. Using fork, toss prunes, nuts, coriander and parsley into couscous.
3 Remove any excess fat from pork. Place pork on board, upside-down; slice through thickest part of pork horizontally, without cutting through at the other side. Open pork out to form one large piece; press approximately 1 cup of the couscous mixture against loin along width of pork. Roll pork to enclose stuffing, securing with kitchen string at 2cm intervals.
4 Place rolled pork on oiled wire rack in large shallow flameproof baking dish; pour 500ml of the cider over pork. Roast, uncovered, 50 minutes or until cooked through. Remove pork from dish; cover to keep warm.
5 Place remaining couscous mixture in small ovenproof dish; cook, covered, in oven about 10 minutes or until heated through.

6 Meanwhile, heat pan juices in baking dish, add remaining cider, apple, onion and sugar; cook, stirring, until apple is just tender.
7 Serve sliced pork with apple mixture and couscous.

prep + cook time 1 hour 35 minutes
serves 4
nutritional count per serving
8.1g total fat (2.0g saturated fat); 727 cal (3044kJ); 111.1g carbohydrate; 32.3g protein; 4.6g fibre

tip To simplify the recipe, ask your butcher to remove any excess fat and butterfly the pork for you.

BAKED HAM WITH REDCURRANT GLAZE

290g redcurrant jelly
2 tablespoons balsamic vinegar
50g brown sugar
3 cloves
8kg leg of ham
250ml water
20 baby onions (600g)

1 Preheat oven to 180°C/160°C fan-assisted.
2 Stir jelly, vinegar, sugar and cloves in medium saucepan over medium heat until sugar is dissolved. Reserve 60ml glaze for the onions.
3 Cut through rind about 10cm from shank end of leg in decorative pattern; run thumb around edge of rind just under skin to remove rind. Start pulling rind from widest edge of ham, continue to pull carefully away from fat up to decorative pattern; discard rind.
4 Using sharp knife, score fat by making shallow cuts diagonally in both directions at 3cm intervals.
5 Place ham on oiled wire rack in a large baking dish; pour in the water. Brush ham all over with glaze. Cover shank end with foil; roast, uncovered, 45 minutes.
6 Meanwhile, add onions to small baking dish with reserved glaze and 2 tablespoons water. Cover with foil; roast with ham for further 45 minutes or until tender. Brush ham with glaze every 30 minutes.
7 Serve ham with onions.

prep + cook time 2 hours
serves 10
nutritional count per serving
33.8g total fat (12.4g saturated fat); 853 cal (3566kJ); 26.8g carbohydrate; 109.1g protein; 1.1g fibre

FISH

SALMON WITH HERB & WALNUT CRUST

1kg piece salmon fillet
1 tablespoon olive oil
6 tablespoons coarsely chopped fresh flat-leaf parsley
3 tablespoons coarsely chopped fresh dill
1 clove garlic, crushed
2 teaspoons finely grated lemon rind
30g coarsely chopped roasted walnuts
2 teaspoons lemon juice
1 tablespoon olive oil, extra

1 Preheat oven to 200°C/180°C fan-assisted.
2 Place salmon in large baking dish; brush with oil. Roast for 5 minutes.
3 Meanwhile, combine remaining ingredients in medium bowl.
4 Remove salmon from oven, sprinkle with three-quarters of the parsley mixture. Roast salmon further 5 minutes. The salmon will be rare in the thicker end of the fillet – you can adjust cooking time to suit your taste.
5 Transfer salmon to serving platter; sprinkle with remaining parsley mixture. Serve with lemon wedges, if desired.

prep + cook time 20 minutes
serves 6
nutritional count per serving
21.4g total fat (3.7g saturated fat); 327 cal (1367kJ); 0.3g carbohydrate; 33.4g protein; 0.7g fibre

tip The salmon can be cooked several hours ahead and served cold, if preferred; otherwise, roast close to serving.

SLOW-ROASTED PESTO SALMON

2 handfuls fresh basil leaves
2 cloves garlic, chopped coarsely
2 tablespoons roasted pine nuts
2 tablespoons lemon juice
60ml olive oil
1.5kg piece salmon fillet, skin on
2 tablespoons olive oil, extra
2 large red peppers (700g),
  chopped coarsely
1 large red onion (300g), chopped
  coarsely

1 Preheat oven to 160°C/140°C fan-assisted.
2 Blend or process basil, garlic, nuts and juice until combined. With motor operating, gradually add oil in thin, steady stream until pesto thickens slightly.
3 Place fish, skin-side down, on piece of oiled foil large enough to completely enclose fish; coat fish with half the pesto. Gather corners of foil together above fish; twist to enclose securely. Place parcel on oven tray; roast about 45 minutes or until cooked as desired.
4 Meanwhile, heat extra oil in large frying pan; cook pepper and onion, stirring, until onion softens.
5 Serve salmon topped with onion mixture and drizzled with remaining pesto.

prep + cook time 1 hour 5 minutes
serves 8
nutritional count per serving
27.5g total fat (4.8g saturated fat); 431 cal (1802kJ); 6.1g carbohydrate; 39.2g protein; 2.0g fibre

TANDOORI SALMON WITH PILAF & RAITA

4 x 200g salmon fillets
70g tandoori curry paste
2 tablespoons natural yogurt
2 teaspoons lemon juice
2 tablespoons groundnut oil
1 large white onion (200g), sliced
2 cloves garlic, sliced
½ teaspoon cumin seeds
½ teaspoon coriander seeds
pinch ground turmeric
300g basmati rice
875ml chicken stock
2 teaspoons grated lemon rind
cucumber & mint raita
½ medium cucumber (75g)
1 tablespoon chopped fresh mint
200g natural yogurt

1 Place salmon in non-metallic dish; pour combined paste, yogurt and juice over fish. (If time permits, cover and refrigerate 2 hours.)
2 Meanwhile, preheat oven to 200°C/180°C fan-assisted.
3 Heat oil in flameproof baking dish; cook onion, garlic and spices, stirring over heat, until onion softens. Add rice; stir until coated with oil. Stir in stock and rind; bring to the boil. Remove from heat, cover tightly with lid or foil; roast in oven 15 minutes.
4 Uncover rice, top with salmon; roast further 8 minutes or until salmon is cooked as desired.
5 Meanwhile, make cucumber and mint raita.
6 Serve salmon with rice and raita; sprinkle with coriander, if desired.
cucumber & mint raita Halve cucumber lengthways; remove and discard seeds. Chop cucumber finely; combine with mint and yogurt in small bowl.

prep + cook time 55 minutes (+ refrigeration)
serves 4
nutritional count per serving
32.2g total fat (7.3g saturated fat); 776 cal (3244kJ); 68.4g carbohydrate; 51.1g protein; 3.6g fibre

FISH IN PROSCIUTTO WITH CAPERS & GARLIC MAYONNAISE

6 x 360g plate-sized white fish
   (any firm, white-fleshed fish is
   suitable)
2 tablespoons finely grated
   lemon rind
5 cloves garlic, sliced thinly
4 handfuls coarsely chopped fresh
   flat-leaf parsley leaves
18 slices thin prosciutto (220g)
1 tablespoon drained capers,
   chopped
garlic mayonnaise
150g mayonnaise
1 tablespoon lemon juice
1 clove garlic, crushed

1 Preheat the oven to 220°C/
200°C fan-assisted. Line oven trays
with baking parchment.
2 Wash cavity of fish under cold
water; pat dry with absorbent
kitchen paper.
3 Combine rind, garlic, and
parsley in medium bowl; fill fish
cavities with parsley mixture.
Wrap three slices of the prosciutto
around each fish.
4 Place fish on trays; bake
15 minutes. Sprinkle capers over
fish; bake further 5 minutes or until
fish is just cooked through.
5 Meanwhile, make the garlic
mayonnaise.
6 Serve fish with mayonnaise and
lemon wedges, if desired.
garlic mayonnaise Combine
ingredients in small bowl.

prep + cook time 35 minutes
serves 6
nutritional count per serving
14.5g total fat (3.1g saturated
fat); 342 cal (1430kJ); 5.7g
carbohydrate; 46.3g protein;
1.6g fibre
tip For this recipe, be sure the
prosciutto is very thinly sliced.

VINE LEAF-WRAPPED OCEAN TROUT WITH BRAISED FENNEL

2 medium fennel bulbs (600g), untrimmed
1 large brown onion (200g), sliced thinly
2 cloves garlic, sliced thinly
1 tablespoon olive oil
60ml orange juice
125ml chicken stock
60ml dry white wine
8 large fresh grapevine leaves
4 x 200g ocean trout fillets
1 tablespoon finely grated orange rind
180g seedless white grapes

1 Preheat oven to 180°C/160°C fan-assisted.
2 Reserve enough frond tips to make 3 tablespoons before trimming fennel bulbs. Slice fennel thinly then combine in large shallow baking dish with onion, garlic, oil, juice, stock and wine. Bake, covered, in oven 30 minutes. Uncover, stir; bake, uncovered, further 20 minutes or until vegetables soften, stirring occasionally.
3 Meanwhile, dip vine leaves in medium saucepan of boiling water for 10 seconds; transfer immediately to medium bowl of iced water. Drain on absorbent paper. Slightly overlap two vine leaves, vein-sides up, on board; centre one fish fillet on leaves, top with a quarter of the rind and a quarter of the reserved frond tips. Fold leaves over to enclose fish. Repeat with remaining leaves, fish, rind and frond tips. Place vine-leaf parcels on oiled oven tray; bake about 15 minutes or until fish is cooked as desired.
4 Stir grapes into hot fennel mixture; stand, covered, 2 minutes before serving with fish.

prep + cook time 1 hour 10 minutes
serves 4
nutritional count per serving
12.5g total fat (2.5g saturated fat); 342 cal (1433kJ); 13.6g carbohydrate; 41.0g protein; 3.8g fibre
tip You can purchase packaged vine leaves packed in brine from Middle-Eastern food stores and some supermarkets; rinse and dry well before using.

CAJUN-SPICED FISH WITH ROASTED CORN SALSA

1 clove garlic, crushed

20g butter, melted

2 teaspoons sweet paprika

½ teaspoon ground cumin

1 teaspoon ground white pepper

¼ teaspoon cayenne pepper

4 x 200g firm white fish fillets

3 trimmed fresh corn cobs (750g)

1 small red onion (100g), chopped coarsely

1 medium avocado (250g), chopped coarsely

250g cherry tomatoes, halved

2 tablespoons lime juice

3 tablespoons coarsely chopped fresh coriander

1 Preheat oven to 220°C/200°C fan-assisted.

2 Combine garlic and butter in small jug; combine spices in small bowl.

3 Place fish on oven tray, brush both sides with garlic mixture, sprinkle with combined spices. Roast, uncovered, about 15 minutes or until browned both sides and cooked as desired.

4 Meanwhile, roast corn on heated oiled grill plate (or grill or barbecue) until browned all over. When corn is just cool enough to handle, cut kernels from cobs with a small, sharp knife.

5 Combine corn kernels in medium bowl with remaining ingredients.

6 Serve fish with salsa.

prep + cook time 40 minutes
serves 4
nutritional count per serving
20.2g total fat (6.4g saturated fat); 494 cal (2065kJ); 25.7g carbohydrate; 48.3g protein; 8.4g fibre

VEGETABLES

ROAST POTATOES

6 floury potatoes (1.3kg),
  peeled, halved horizontally
2 tablespoons olive oil

1 Preheat oven to 220°C/200°C fan-assisted. Oil oven tray.
2 Boil, steam or microwave potatoes 5 minutes; drain. Pat dry with absorbent paper; cool 10 minutes.
3 Gently rake rounded sides of potatoes with tines of fork; place in single layer, cut-side down, on tray. Brush potatoes with oil.
4 Roast potatoes, uncovered, 50 minutes or until browned and crisp.

prep + cook time 1 hour 5 minutes (+ cooling)
serves 4
nutritional count per serving
9.4g total fat (1.3g saturated fat); 254 cal (1062kJ); 34.1g carbohydrate; 6.2g protein; 4.2g fibre
tips Gently raking the potatoes with a fork aids crisping. Don't crowd the potatoes as they will brown unevenly; ensure the oven has reached the correct temperature before the tray goes in. King Edward, desiree and maris piper are all good for roasting.

ROSEMARY POTATOES

3kg desiree potatoes
2 tablespoons olive oil
1 tablespoon fresh rosemary
  leaves

1 Preheat oven to 180°C/160°C fan-assisted.

2 Make 1cm cuts in each potato, slicing about three-quarters of the way through.

3 Combine potatoes with oil in large baking dish, sprinkle with salt and freshly ground black pepper. Roast about 1 hour.

4 Increase oven temperature to 220°C/200°C fan-assisted. Roast potatoes further 15 minutes or until browned and tender. Sprinkle with rosemary.

prep + cook time 1 hour 35 minutes
serves 10
nutritional count per serving
3.9g total fat (0.5g saturated fat); 193 cal (807kJ); 31.4g carbohydrate; 5.8g protein; 3.8g fibre

HASSELBACK POTATOES

6 desiree potatoes (1.1kg),
    peeled, halved horizontally
40g butter, melted
2 tablespoons olive oil
25g packaged breadcrumbs
60g finely grated cheddar cheese

1 Preheat oven to 180°C/160°C fan-assisted.
2 Place one potato half, cut-side down, on chopping board; place a chopstick on board along each side of potato. Slice potato thinly, cutting down to chopsticks to prevent cutting all the way through. Repeat with remaining potato halves.
3 Coat potato halves in combined butter and oil in medium baking dish; place, rounded-side up, in single layer. Roast, uncovered, 45 minutes, brushing frequently with oil mixture. Continue roasting without brushing about 15 minutes or until potatoes are cooked through.
4 Sprinkle combined breadcrumbs and cheese over potatoes; roast, uncovered, about 10 minutes or until topping is browned lightly.

prep + cook time 1 hour 30 minutes
serves 4
nutritional count per serving 22.8g total fat (10.0g saturated fat); 384 cal (1605kJ); 33.0g carbohydrate; 10.0g protein; 3.8g fibre

MAPLE-GLAZED SWEET POTATOES & RED ONIONS

4 medium sweet potatoes (1.6kg)
2 tablespoons lemon juice
4 medium red onions (680g),
    quartered
2 tablespoons olive oil
2 tablespoons maple syrup
sea salt flakes

1 Preheat oven to 180°C/160°C fan-assisted. Line shallow oven tray with baking parchment.
2 Peel sweet potatoes; place in bowl of cold water with lemon juice to prevent browning. Cut sweet potatoes into thick slices, return to lemon water.
3 Drain sweet potato, pat dry with absorbent paper. Place sweet potato and onion on tray. Drizzle vegetables with oil; drizzle sweet potato only with maple syrup. Sprinkle with salt.
4 Roast vegetables about 40 minutes or until tender and browned.

prep + cook time 55 minutes
serves 8
nutritional count per serving
4.8g total fat (0.6g saturated fat); 223 cal (932kJ); 38.6g carbohydrate; 3.6g protein; 4.5g fibre

ROAST POTATO, ONION & RED PEPPER SALAD

1kg new potatoes, halved
1 medium red onion (170g),
    cut into thin wedges
1 large red pepper (350g),
    chopped coarsely
2 teaspoons olive oil
80g baby rocket leaves
300g can red kidney beans,
    rinsed, drained
100g low-fat feta, diced into
    1cm pieces
2 tablespoons coarsely chopped
    fresh flat-leaf parsley
honey balsamic dressing
1 tablespoon honey
2 teaspoons balsamic vinegar
2 teaspoons water
2 teaspoons olive oil

1 Preheat oven to 220°C/200°C fan-assisted.
2 Combine potato, onion, pepper and oil in large deep baking dish; roast, uncovered, about 40 minutes or until vegetables are browned and tender, stirring halfway through cooking time.
3 Place ingredients for honey balsamic dressing in screw-top jar; shake well.
4 Place roasted vegetables in large bowl with rocket, beans, cheese, parsley and dressing; toss gently to combine.

prep + cook time 55 minutes
serves 4
nutritional count per serving
9.1g total fat (3.0g saturated fat); 359 cal (1501kJ); 50.5g carbohydrate; 17.9g protein; 9.4g fibre

ROASTED TOMATOES WITH GARLIC & HERBS

9 large plum tomatoes (810g), halved
1 teaspoon sea salt
1 teaspoon cracked black pepper
8 sprigs fresh thyme
2 cloves garlic, sliced thinly
60ml olive oil
2 teaspoons finely chopped fresh oregano
1 teaspoon finely chopped fresh thyme

1 Preheat oven to 200°C/180°C fan-assisted.
2 Place tomatoes, cut-side up, in single layer, in large baking dish. Sprinkle with combined salt, pepper, thyme sprigs, garlic and 1 tablespoon of the oil; roast, uncovered, about 1 hour or until tomato softens and browns lightly.
3 Drizzle tomato with combined chopped herbs and remaining oil.

prep + cook time 1 hour 10 minutes
serves 6
nutritional count per serving
9.3g total fat (1.3g saturated fat); 102 cal (426kJ); 2.7g carbohydrate; 1.4g protein; 1.8g fibre
tip roast the tomatoes in a baking dish with deep sides; this will shield them from the heat so they won't burn.

ROASTED BABY CARROTS WITH GARLIC

3 bunches baby carrots (1kg)
60ml olive oil
2 cloves garlic, crushed
2 teaspoons honey
1 tablespoon fresh thyme leaves

1 Preheat oven to 220°C/200°C fan-assisted.
2 Trim carrot tops, leaving 2cm of the stems intact. Wash carrots well.
3 Place carrots in medium baking dish with combined oil, garlic and honey; toss well. Roast, uncovered, 15 minutes.
4 Add thyme leaves and roast further 3 minutes or until tender.

prep + cook time 35 minutes
serves 10
nutritional count per serving
5.6g total fat (0.8g saturated fat); 82 cal (343kJ); 6.0g carbohydrate; 0.7g protein; 3.0g fibre

ROAST BEETROOT & ONION

2 tablespoons olive oil
10 medium unpeeled fresh
  beetroot (1.6kg), halved
20 baby onions (500g), peeled
2 tablespoons red wine vinegar
2 tablespoons olive oil, extra
2 tablespoons coarsely chopped
  flat-leaf parsley

1 Preheat oven to 240°C/220°C fan-assisted.
2 Brush base of baking dish with half of the oil, add beetroot; cover tightly with foil. Roast 45 minutes.
3 Combine onions with remaining oil, add to beetroot; cover tightly with foil. Roast 30 minutes or until tender. Remove foil; roast further 10 minutes.
4 Wearing rubber gloves, remove skin from hot beetroot; cut beetroot in half. Place beetroot and onion in serving dish; drizzle with combined vinegar and extra oil, sprinkle with parsley and freshly ground black pepper.

prep + cook time 1 hour 50 minutes
serves 6
nutritional count per serving
12.5g total fat (1.7g saturated fat); 237 cal (991kJ); 21.9g carbohydrate; 5.5g protein; 8.0g fibre

MIXED GARLIC MUSHROOMS

500g flat mushrooms
80ml olive oil
500g chestnut mushrooms
500g button mushrooms
2 cloves garlic, sliced thinly
6 tablespoons flat-leaf parsley
  leaves

1 Preheat oven to 200°C/180°C fan-assisted.
2 Place flat mushrooms in large baking dish, drizzle with half of the oil; roast, uncovered, 10 minutes.
3 Add remaining mushrooms, oil and garlic to dish; roast, uncovered, further 15 minutes or until mushrooms are tender and browned lightly. Stir in parsley.

prep + cook time 30 minutes
serves 10
nutritional count per serving
7.8g total fat (1.0g saturated fat); 100 cal (418kJ); 0.5g carbohydrate; 5.5g protein; 4.0g fibre

HOW TO CARVE

The first requisite for all carving is a razor-sharp knife. Ideally, it should be long, narrow and slightly flexible. It is easier to carve on a board than on a platter, as the meat won't slip. The board should have a channel to catch the juices.

All meat consists of muscles in which bundles of fibres run in one direction, and you should carve across the fibres (across the grain), not along them. This makes all the difference to the texture of the meat, as short lengths of fibre feel tender to eat while long ones feel chewy and tough.

CHICKEN & TURKEY

Cut off the wing then the hindquarter on the same side, cutting through the thigh bone.

Turn the bird on its side; place the cut-off wing and hindquarter under the bird to help keep it steady

Holding the bird firmly with a fork, carve across the breast at the top, running along the bird's torso.

Carve the leg and wing then turn the bird over and carve the other side in the same manner.

HAM

Cut a circle through the rind at the bone end; run your fingers around the edge, pull the rind back from the cut.

To begin carving, cut a small wedge from the top of the ham close to the remaining rind on the bone end.

Make long sweeps with the knife to get large thin slices. As you carve, the slices will increase in size.

As you continue slicing, the ham can be adjusted on the stand so it can be carved from the side.

GLOSSARY

almonds
ground also known as almond meal; nuts are powdered to a coarse flour texture.
slivered cut lengthways.
bok choy also called pak choi or Chinese chard; has a mild mustard taste and is good braised or in stir-fries. Baby bok choy is also available.
brazil nuts native to South America, a triangular-shelled oily nut with an unusually tender white flesh and a mild, rich flavour. Good for eating as well as cooking, the nuts can be eaten raw or cooked, or can be ground into meal for baking.
breadcrumbs
packaged fine-textured, purchased white breadcrumbs.
stale one- or two-day-old bread made into crumbs by grating, blending or processing.
capers the grey-green buds of a warm climate shrub sold either dried and salted or pickled in vinegar brine.
cheese
cheddar the most common cow's milk cheese; should be aged and hard.
parmesan a sharp-tasting, dry, hard cheese, made from skimmed or semi-skimmed milk and aged for at least a year.

ricotta a soft, sweet, moist, white, cow's milk cheese with a low fat content (about 8.5 per cent) and a slightly grainy texture. The name roughly translates as 'cooked again' and refers to ricotta's manufacture from a whey that is itself a by-product of other cheese making.
chinese cooking wine a clear distillation of fermented rice, water and salt, it's about 29.5% alcohol by volume. Used for marinades and as a sauce ingredient, it can be purchased from most Asian food stores.
chorizo a sausage of Spanish origin; made of coarsely ground pork and seasoned with garlic and chillies.
cornflour also known as cornstarch; used as a thickening agent in cooking.
couscous a fine, grain-like cereal product, made from semolina.
cream we used fresh cream in this book, unless otherwise stated. Also known as single cream and pouring cream; has no additives unlike commercially thickened cream. Minimum fat content 35%.
crème fraîche a mature fermented cream (minimum fat content 35%) having a slightly tangy flavour and velvety rich texture; similar thickness to soured cream.

fennel bulb vegetable, also known as finocchio or anise. Also the name given to dried seeds having a liquorice flavour.
five-spice powder a fragrant mixture of ground cinnamon, cloves, star anise, sichuan pepper and fennel seeds.
horseradish a vegetable having edible green leaves but mainly grown for its long, pungent white root. Some Asian food shops sell it fresh, but it's more common sold in bottles at the supermarket in two forms: prepared horseradish (preserved grated horseradish) and horseradish cream (a creamy paste made of grated horseradish, vinegar, oil and sugar). They cannot be substituted for each other in cooking but are both used as table condiments.
kalonji seeds also known as nigella or black onion seeds. Tiny, angular seeds, black on the outside and a creamy colour within, with a sharp nutty flavour that can be enhanced by frying briefly in a dry hot pan before use. Are available in most supermarkets. Often called black cumin seeds.
macadamias native to Australia, a rich and buttery nut; store in refrigerator because of its high oil content.

maple syrup sweet syrup distilled from the sap of maple trees found only in Canada and parts of North America where it is popular on pancakes. Maple-flavoured syrup is not an adequate substitute for the real thing.

mushrooms

button small, cultivated white mushrooms having a delicate, subtle flavour.

chestnut light to dark brown mushrooms with mild, earthy flavour.

enoki also known as enokitake; grown and bought in clumps, these delicately-flavoured mushrooms have small cream caps on long thin stalks. Available from Asian food shops and supermarkets.

flat a mushroom with a rich earthy flavour; sometimes misnamed field mushrooms.

shimeji grey in colour with a rich spicy flavour; good eaten in salads.

mustard

dijon a pale brown, distinctively flavoured fairly mild French mustard.

wholegrain also known as seeded. A French-style coarse-grain mustard made from crushed mustard seeds and dijon-style French mustard.

olives

black have a richer and more mellow flavour than the green variety and are softer in texture. Sold either plain or in a piquant marinade.

green those harvested before fully ripened and are, as a rule, denser and more bitter than their black relatives.

onions

brown an all-purpose onion, with a light brown skin and yellow flesh.

red a sweet-flavoured, large, purple-red onion.

orzo pasta small, rice-shaped pasta; used in soups and salads

pancetta an Italian salt-cured pork roll, usually cut from the belly; used, chopped, in cooked dishes to add flavours. Bacon can be substituted.

paprika ground dried red bell pepper; available sweet, smoked or hot. Sweet paprika is available at delis, speciality food stores and on line.

pine nuts also known as pignoli; small, cream-coloured kernels obtained from the cones of different varieties of pine trees.

poussin a small chicken, no more than 6 weeks old, weighing a maximum 500g.

redcurrant jelly a sweet condiment traditionally served with lamb or poultry.

sesame seeds black and white are the most common of these tiny oval seeds; a good source of calcium.

star anise a dried star-shaped pod, the seeds of which taste of aniseed.

soy sauce made from fermented soy beans; several variations are available.

sweet potato fleshy root vegetable; available with red or white flesh.

tamarind concentrate the tamarind tree produces clusters of hairy brown pods, each of which is filled with seeds and a viscous pulp, that are dried and pressed into the blocks of tamarind concentrate. Releases a sweet-sour, slightly astringent taste. Available from delis, Asian and Indian supermarkets and on line.

tandoori paste Indian blend of hot and fragrant spices including turmeric, paprika, chilli powder, saffron, cardamom and garam masala.

tomato paste triple-concentrated tomato purée used to flavour soups, stews, sauces and casseroles.

vinegar

balsamic authentic only from the province of Modena, Italy; made from a regional wine of white trebbiano grapes specially processed then aged in antique wooden casks to give the exquisite pungent flavour.

red wine based on fermented red wine.

white wine based on fermented white wine.

walnuts large nut with distinctive ridged kernels. Walnuts contain the beneficial omega-3 fatty acids, which is terrific news for people who dislike the taste of fish.

yogurt an unflavoured, full-fat cows' milk yogurt has been used in these recipes unless otherwise stated.

INDEX

CONVERSION CHARTS

measures

One metric tablespoon holds 20ml; one metric teaspoon holds 5ml.

All cup and spoon measurements are level. The most accurate way of measuring dry ingredients is to weigh them. When measuring liquids, use a clear glass or plastic jug with metric markings.

We use large eggs with an average weight of 60g.

dry measures

METRIC	IMPERIAL
15g	½oz
30g	1oz
60g	2oz
90g	3oz
125g	4oz (¼lb)
155g	5oz
185g	6oz
220g	7oz
250g	8oz (½lb)
280g	9oz
315g	10oz
345g	11oz
375g	12oz (¾lb)
410g	13oz
440g	14oz
470g	15oz
500g	16oz (1lb)
750g	24oz (1½lb)
1kg	32oz (2lb)

liquid measures

METRIC	IMPERIAL
30ml	1 fluid oz
60ml	2 fluid oz
100ml	3 fluid oz
125ml	4 fluid oz
150ml	5 fluid oz
190ml	6 fluid oz
250ml	8 fluid oz
300ml	10 fluid oz
500ml	16 fluid oz
600ml	20 fluid oz
1000ml (1 litre)	32 fluid oz

length measures

3mm	⅛in
6mm	¼in
1cm	½in
2cm	¾in
2.5cm	1in
5cm	2in
6cm	2½in
8cm	3in
10cm	4in
13cm	5in
15cm	6in
18cm	7in
20cm	8in
23cm	9in
25cm	10in
28cm	11in
30cm	12in (1ft)

oven temperatures

These are fan-assisted temperatures. If you have a conventional oven (ie. not fan-assisted), increase temperatures by 10–20°.

	°C (CELSIUS)	°F (FAHRENHEIT)	GAS MARK
Very low	100	210	½
Low	130	260	1–2
Moderately low	140	280	3
Moderate	160	325	4–5
Moderately hot	180	350	6
Hot	200	400	7–8
Very hot	220	425	9